JOY IS
THE THINNEST LAYER

Joy is
the Thinnest Layer

Gunilla Norris

HOMEBOUND
PUBLICATIONS
Independent Publisher of Contemplative Titles
STONINGTON, CONNECTICUT

FIRST EDITION TRADE PAPERBACK
ISBN: 978-1-938846-65-6 (PBK)

Published in 2016 by Homebound Publications
Book Designed by Leslie M. Browning
Cover Images © Steve Heap

Library of Congress Cataloging-in-Publication Data

Names: Norris, Gunilla, 1939- author.
Title: Joy is the thinnest layer / by Gunilla Norris.
Description: First edition trade paperback. | Pawcatuck, Connecticut : Homebound Publications, 2016.
Identifiers: LCCN 2016003853 | ISBN 9781938846656 (paperback)
Classification: LCC PS3564.O646 A6 2016 | DDC 811/.54--DC23
LC record available at http://lccn.loc.gov/2016003853

10 9 8 7 6 5 4 3 2

Homebound Publications is committed to ecological stewardship. We greatly value the natural environment and invests in environmental conservation. Our books are printed on paper with chain of custody certification from the Forest Stewardship Council, Sustainable Forestry Initiative, and the Program for the Endorsement of Forest Certification.

For Stanley

Acknowledgements

My gratitude goes to Joanie McLean, wonderful partner in poetry, for her thoughtful reading of this book and her valuable suggestions. So, too, to Greta Sibley, long time beloved collaborator, for her insightful and continual help. My thanks to Mary Ann Hoberman, Florence Phillips and Jane Milliken, dear friends, who all read the book and helped me see it more clearly. And, of course, my special editor, Leslie M. Browning for her belief in this book.

TABLE OF CONTENTS

Then, Is It Now?

About Love

Every Day

FOREWORD

When this book is published I will be seventy-seven years old. That is old but not ancient. When you are in your later years it is natural to consider your life and to look at it in depth. What has been lived and learned?

There is a fluidity that can be felt between the past and the present. For me they somehow merge into a single now where a thin layer is lifted to reveal experience in its on going pain, joy and beauty. The reader can perhaps perceive that the different sections of the book consider a core place or "home" I was living from and so sense how the parts might connect.

"Then, is it Now?" is about growing up and leaving home. "About Love" is explained by the title. My partner of many years has had Parkinson's disease, and as the illness progresses we have found ourselves homebound. When one is homebound introspection comes about easily, and so that very fact has set me to the task of assembling the poems of this book. Some of them are more than thirty years old.

"Every Day" is about the gift of living. How fleeting and timeless is a single day. One by one we must let our days go no matter how wonderful or dreadful they are. To feel free and at home in impermanence and to revere the gift of experience is an ongoing soul task.

Gunilla Norris
Mystic, CT, 2015

THEN, IS IT NOW?

GATE-SWINGING

On the sofa, with the light not yet on
I drift. Half awake, it's hard to know
where I am in the deepening dusk.

I've grown old. My breath is a soft mauve.

The wind picks up a shutter, moves it.
I hear it out there, insistent and rusty
as if a mute were trying to speak.

What is here in this half-light?

The sound takes me
to the far pasture, back to the old gate
I used to ride when I was young.

To open it was exultation.

I clung, blue-fingered to the weathered firs.
Winter was inside the heartwood of that lumber.
The gate swung, moaning until it met the latch.

It had a weight of sorrow.

Could it be I am still there?
Wind on my face? Air electric.
hanging on in a kind of fear-joy?

Against my chest I feel the heartwood.

Ore Trees, the loggers call them
from the metal sound the axe makes
when they are felled. Each one contains
more silence than any human life can bear.

STITCHING

I

She wished to be a nurse,
carry a black bag on dusty roads
to the out-lying villages beyond the manor.
She wanted to eat simple fare:
boiled potatoes, hard rye bread, pickled herring—
the people's food. She wanted to be of help.
This was not seemly in those days.

She must marry her kind
and live appropriately with little love
perhaps, but at least with the family silver,
cut glasses, parquet floors and
exact monograms carefully stitched
through days of longing. She married.
There were five children,

each with children. I am one of those,
and learned my stitching from her.
The years pass, the clocks tick.
Needles enter the cloth—
she leaves her mark, initials
embossed in silk on woven flax,
grown there near the dusty roads.

II

Morning. Grandmother is in bed
under white linen. Her long hair falls
over the small red crosses
stitched on the collar of her night shift.
We know this hair after breakfast,
in a perfect twist, not a strand out of place.
But now it flows like water across the covers.

Grandfather has already died
when this takes place. We are three
girls, under twelve, watching
Grandmother's belly as it rises and falls.
She is telling us a story. We laugh
a little afraid of the strangeness, the way
she looks as if she were from another place.

Still, for a while, she is herself, belly dancing
until she does not belong to us any more and
we begin to smell something foreign. What is it?
Kid roasting over charcoal? Sounds? Bleating?
Bells? Yes! The wail of strange instruments,
and clapping, too. Men cry out in approval.
Where could we be? We look down

to find where we stand. In throbbing music
our bare feet dance on packed ground.
We are stamping and turning.
There's a ring on one of our toes with a stone.
It's small, an open eye catching light. As we turn
and turn it shimmers and our veils lift
in the brown dust of a possible world.

III

Grandmother is playing Chopin in the dark.
She doesn't need the music. She knows the notes
by heart. I lean my head against the piano.
On the floor I can see the reflected fringe
from the tablecloth. It's a shadow fence

keeping darkness out, or are we prisoners
kept in? I can feel hammers
strike the strings and my temple.
When pain is a known comfort, there is truce.
The prisoners walk out to watch

the same moon with the guard,
feed the same impromptu fire.
The mournful notes are merry
and very precise. They touch everything.
For a moment we feel known.

IV

In the humming of bees
we've slipped away, becoming the same
age, Grandmother and I. No gold bands on our fingers.
Small houses lie scattered haphazardly
where they were hammered
into the landscape. We saunter
as green summer smells seep out
from under the hedgerows. Through
an open window we hear a toddler wail:
the next generation turns red
with discomfort and rage.
A white curtain flutters. Above us

larks soar into the thinnest air.
No one tells us what to do.
We aren't in anyone's story.
Not even our own. Belonging to no one
we whistle, kick stones into ditches. Free.
Then the radio crackles. News. Clocks
start ticking again. We fall back
into the present, into the living room where
Grandmother sits quietly in her chair. Frail,
she will die this year. Her patient face has already turned
that way. The road lies open, luminous . . .
a silk thread like the others, pulled without breaking.

They Went North

I

Grandmother is first in the pew.
Her stillness folds over itself like cloth.
We come next—a pack of cousins,
hot and sticky. Grandfather is last.

Body heat steams in our jackets.
Snow-mud drips on the floor.
Stop scuffing!!
Time groans inside us.

This place belongs to Grandmother and we belong to her.

II

Lumber was Grandfather's work.
As newlyweds they went north,
settled on the last stop of the railway.
There was only pine, stone
and birch after that.

She was alone without music.

He marked trees meant for cutting.
Soon children came, five,
and the mudroom filled
with boots and wet wool—
more isolation.

One moonless night the black ice cracked.

She was flooded, began to grow
flowers in meager light,
asked for a piano,
silk thread from the city.
God-space opened inside her.

She embroidered a cloth

for the altar . . . white on white
on white . . . embossed,
packed solid with stitches—
her needles leaving tracks
on that wintry ground.

III

Above us the minister's bee voice
hovers and drones. It's 40 years later.
We fidget in the pew.

Then the man comes for the collection.
Grandfather winks and hands us our buttons.
Into the pouch they go. Plop... Plop...

We are caught, unable to refuse this offering
from Grandmother's button box to God.
The sun creeps in through the window.

The altar cloth drapes
over the polished wood,
a white wing. At night

we think it lifts and flies
out through the window. Bells
ring in the frosty air.

We stand. Praise God
from whom all blessings flow.
On the floor the mud puddles glisten.

Anything can happen.

It's exactly noon.

OBSERVATION

From here we can see forever.
It's the middle of August. Already fall.

Everything is burning.

Grandfather parks his blunderbuss
and sinks down on a stone.
He has thickened over the years
and is tired from our climb above the tree line.
With a big ham of a hand he pats his pants pocket
and gazes out over blue distances.

Water or Cognac? he hollers into the wind.

The voice is confident. As we know
it will, the echo returns. Cognac. Cognac.
Right, he says and takes the pewter plunta
out of his pocket. He is diabetic and
this is a forbidden swig. Still

a man must live in his own way, free from the carefulness of women.

The wind's stray dog nips our fingers.
In a week or two, the first flurries. Already
the light has gone down into scree and moss.
There's only a little time left for this generation.

Over the high, bare ridges a herd of reindeer threads its way

like a string of dark beads. The Lapps are moving
to winter quarters. This trek is annual.
Grandfather jabs me and points.
We love this mystery of others
in the wild without official observation.

The herd moves out of sight. We wait.

It's only a few decades
before a new wind blows, bringing
acid rain, then Chernobyl. Officials
arrive with regulations and papers.
They can go anywhere in their shiny snowmobiles.

Then radioactive roundups—mandatory reindeer slaughter.

Grandfather sits under the leaded lamp suspended
from the ceiling. Eerie green light falls on his face. In the end
too much change and the inevitable happens–a move south
to the city. I can't touch him anymore. When I try, he says,
You have butter on your fingers, shuffles cards,
deals them out one by one, carefully in order.

CROSSING

I

Bits of seaweed float just under the surface.
A soft shuddering hums up through my feet,
massive propellers churn, the boat is alive.
Water begins to boil like soup. Down below
everyone is dressed in white. Handkerchiefs,

also white, fly back and forth like sea gulls
in a feeding frenzy. I am four and a half
and cling to the railing. Everything is interesting
and sad. My nanny dabs her face,
and I see how her shoulders shake.

A taxi pulls up. A man arrives late for good-byes,
sprints over the silver-gray boards of the jetty. *Hallo,*
he cries. A shimmering, red box of chocolates hurtles towards us.
For a second it hangs there in the air, makes a quarter turn
and plunges into the water. Bubbles rise to the surface.

The box has many layers.
We are saying our good-byes,
sailing east through minefields, north to home.
The box keeps sinking.
Slowly the bubbles grow smaller and smaller.

II

Overcast days. Water, scaled and shiny, rises and falls
as if great beasts breathed just under the surface.
We steam forward, through them, with guide wires
stretched to four minesweepers, two on each side.
On deck the crew stands in their white hats and trousers,
rifles at the ready.

The wind gathers.
Tablecloths, heavy and damp, keep our plates in place.
Tables skate away from the chairs. Later . . . everything falls.
We're too startled to cry. Somewhere in London, or
perhaps a city in Belgium, a child sees the bed
with her sleeping parents, fall into night. Falling, falling . . .

we're blown from our course. The wind screeches.
Atlantic swells hiss over the wheelhouse. Trembling,
father holds my hand. Years ago, off a sand bar
in Mar del Plata, he and his friend were pulled
out beyond their strength. The friend drowned,
but father was swept back to shore, back to my mother's fires.

His face is white. Eyes bore into me. *You were conceived in this—*
fire and water. *Do not give up*, he whispers as we're hurled
against the dark teak of the wainscoting, against each other.
He is talking to himself. *Never give up. It is possible to live!*
We have missed the rendezvous with our convoy.
The sextant is broken. The sky's thick and black. No stars.

III

Morning dawns in a haze and sea spume. Impossible
to know where we are. In the mist the freighter wallows
idly. We wait for a cloudless night, wait for stars.
When the waves settle, the mines are sighted.
Guns pop and sputter over the sides. For days
we are rocked by detonations. Then silence.
Smoke blows over us . . . dark migrating birds.

In France they have rubble. A bombed church spire,
with its clock still ticking, points to the earth
where we cannot live together. A young
crewmember sights along his weapon. He could be a man
with a spear on a Viking ship or someone more ancient,
someone with nothing but a blunt stone in his hand.
The motto: To be sure. Kill.

Sweat glistens in the stubble on the sailor's chin.
I see it from the lifeboats where I've found a perch.
Flocks of flying fish bounce up out of the water,
frolicking. Something lives. They scud past us,
diving down, pulsing up. The war has not touched them.
The cloud-cloth shreds and tares. Tonight,
a sky with Orion's belt, his flickering knife.

IV

Something slips in close. Everyone dashes to the railing.
A collective in-breath. *Mine!* shouts the sailor.
I creep forward to see. We gaze at a green island,
mottled and pocked, rocking in the waves.
Yes, a mine. Perhaps not. Perhaps
something else? A turtle? It lifts its head.
The small, black eyes above the beak look at me.

With thick trusting wings its curved legs fly slowly
through the water, through my mind. Something lives.
Beside me the guns are readied. If I don't look, perhaps
they'll not shoot. I have seen him. He has seen me.
Only that second! Now I want the great turtle
to dive into the depths. I hurl my hope down.
They shoot.

V

Without lights we're a ghost ship sliding through
the North Sea. The coasts, too, are without lights.
We're kept in silence, live-wired. For now
we're just a black hulk passing for an outlying skerry.
Almost home. In the hold a box of oranges has sprung apart.
The smell of rotting fruit wafts up to our beds
into our dreams. We will arrive undetected.

In that deep water, that one second, there were bubbles.
We travel north, now by land. There,
even at three in the afternoon, it is dark.
Our hands and faces are greased with pig fat against the cold.
Boots lined with newspapers, we walk on war reports,
body counts, the first hints, more like hopes
that the war will soon be over. Dimly we see

to play in a yard of snow where igloo lanterns glow
with hoarded candle stumps. Around us the trees crowd in.
The cold is metallic. Fire and frozen water.
Great northern lights flare over our heads.
They could be the green smoke of crematoria or the dawn.
We cling to our small lights—not knowing, not ever knowing
and what can be born in that.

KEEPING WARM

Our feet press against heated stones
placed under bear fur   It's winter
We sway back and forth

in the horse drawn sled   Trees
pass us on either side   Stillness
expands in the jingle of harness bells

It is 1943   Snow covers everything
The war wants our pink lungs
We try not to breathe the cold   The dead

bear skin keeps us   Close and together
we rock over the bleak blue-black ruts
Breath-clouds cover our faces

O

I

A grass O
is the green period
the road's long sentence makes at the front of the manor.

Around it, gravel is raked every day into scalloped sweeps
we must not walk on. Shooed away birds,
we scatter into the trees. On the property:

wooden barn, wash house, weaving house, bath house, play house with
wood stove. We play with blue plates from the East India Company.
It's near the middle of the twentieth century, and we're learning

to be seen but not heard. Every day
Great Grandmother holds prayer—staff and family.
She plays the spinet. We sing, read the Bible. This is law.

Later we eat in the kitchen with the servants.
I want to be out in the light,
away from the starched aprons.

I want to be by the river's edge,
sit on the bath house steps, watch the water eddy
and swirl. Mid-stream is my stone. The first goal . . .

O . . . to swim there.

Great Grandmother doesn't come to the water any more.
She's too old. Instead she rules from the parlor and account books.
Close by bees hum in their white boxes. I understand I'm alone.

II

Fall.

We are in our school desks, wiggling.
Everyone has worms. It's epidemic.

Fresh food is scarce. The days are long.

Alphabet cards hang above the blackboard.
I gaze at the one in which a snake bites its tail.

The forked tongue draws me in. I glide
into the O. It is the first moment

I read.

III

Siren wails sweep through the city.
We pull the blinds, turn out lights,

go under something solid. We're practicing
in case the war might take a different turn.

In the Baltic, German U-boats glint like minnows
in the shallows. They can hear everything.

Further south, German troops march or ride
through Skåne on the way to Denmark and Norway,

our neighbors. We are neutral and collaborate.
There are trains jammed with soldiers.

The moon is full. O. Mother brings a candle.
Life has to go on by one light or another.

We climb into our beds. Without face or name,
we hear something howl and cry in the night.

IV

My friend and I run
down from Maria Kyrkan
with its tall black steeple to the pet shop.

It's after school.

We hurry because the shop will close soon.
We've come to see the puppies, a month old.
We are in love dreaming against window glass.

We do not notice the cold or the bells tolling the hour.

The shop attendant draws the blind. *Closed.*

I turn then and see, before it's true, the black
mourning band on my friend's sleeve.

Small stitches hold the grief in place.

Drawn behind a white blind
her mother will be swallowed in an avalanche.
The O, darker on the faded coat sleeve, still remains

when the threads are snipped. Silently

my friend is marked.
We light what remains of our candles. Burning,
the orphan stumps illuminate what is already dark.

V

I dream chestnut trees in the churchyard
where we play mumbelipeg on the gravel paths.

My knife, a treasure stolen from the back of the drawer,
is sharp from afternoons of concentration. We know

how to make our squares, throw our pitch, divide the space,
take possession. We are doing the common work of nations—

what you take, you may keep, for a while
among gravestones with their yellow lichen.

We sharpen our knives clickety clack, clickety clack
against the wrought iron that holds the dead in their places.

We hear the church bell, look up as the clapper swings
and sounds in its heavy brass O.

Rooks burst out of the belfry. Sweeping,
they cut up the air with their black wings.

TALK

I have always been faithful, he says.

Do you believe me? The question is solemn.

I'm there in the brown leather sofa, eleven
and sleepy. It's almost two in the morning.

Having been wakened again, I hug myself.
Father talks at me from behind his desk for an hour.

Here is where I learn to listen.

I gaze at the two large tumblers
leaving sweat on the blotter.

Cigarette smoke hangs like tent cloth from the ceiling.
I love her, he mumbles, meaning mother. *I love her*

. . . trying to keep it that way though his doubts hover
in the smoke. I listen.

Outside the night is thick and somehow sullen.
I am tired. He will talk and talk.

My mother, asleep in their bedroom, doesn't know
that he wakes me, doesn't know, the way I do,

that the gun is in the closet, that I will hunt for
the bullets, keep the lethal secrets hidden

in my school socks. Deep in my chest
the small, black seeds of their grief sprout my future.

WAITING

We wait for the trawlers
coming in from the hazy North Sea.

The three of us dangle our legs over weathered boards
and hear the glub, glub of the incoming tide.

With money in our pockets for dinner,
we've been sent out for the evening,

suddenly old enough to roam around town.
My sister has the watch and is in charge

with instructions: to be away at least three hours.
Our parents, in some desperate embrace, are locked away

behind the door of their hotel room.
We won't know our fate till it opens

. . . will they emerge together or apart?
We wait out here as the sun sets,

all three keepers of time. The ticking
sound of the diesel engines grows louder.

Smell of tar and oil. We stand up, eager to watch men
maneuver boats up against the docks. Heavy, they glide in,

are lashed down, then secured in one continuous movement.
The men grunt, *En bra dag*. A good day.

We hand them grown-up money, fingers sweating
around the silver coins. Three kroner apiece,

enough for a hefty bag of prawns
boiled in seawater. We eat them.

The peels, pale as fingernails,
fall from our hands into the shallows.

From time to time my sister looks at her watch.
Below us the tide is full.

Slate-colored the water is strewn with our litter.
We watch the waves take the shells into shore

and out again, back and forth as if unable to decide
where to put them. We are transparent,

naked without skins, growing older
as the second hand moves in its circle.

LEAVING HOME

So quietly in time
am I woven

Through days and hours
the shuttle flies

a dark bird
on an errand   It carries

the thread back and forth
The fabric grows every hour

I'm fashioned by
interlocking threads   Shaped

and colored   Wild and abandoned
beach rose   Wince-red

flame of sumac   Blue
forget-me-not   Everything noticed

even the silver scissors
that cut me free

from the loom   Softly they whisper
A sound of skin severed from skin

COMING TO LIGHT

I

We've taken the bus down to the wharf—
a great effort—and walked to the high wall
behind which the Atlantic hurls itself on the rocks.
Mother leans against the thick concrete
eagerly sucking in the salty mist.
How many times has she scanned her horizon,
that place she cannot see beyond?

Härligheten, in here, she points to her chest
where the lungs are wrecked from early bouts of TB.
But she means the glory of light making its way
through layers, making its way out from everything.
How did I not know we had come to the time
of countable breaths? The last day
and its shimmer.

II

Mother sketches. Quick and sure,
the blunt pencil moves on the inside
of a book of matches, catching light
or movement, finding joy right next to the red
utility matches. Perhaps her heart burst in the night

because the sunny ocean winked at her too many times,
or the café's umbrellas were so intensely lime green
against the gray cliffs to be unbearable, or that
the tiny espresso cups were brown eyes filled full
of the deepest liquid. No way to see bottom.

Her fingers are on fire without striking anything.
She gives herself to the point of the pencil—the place
where the sea pounds the cliffs, where the lead touches
the paper, where line and curve are one, where
the love that never left her is, and she died living it.

III

At the bus stop ready to return.
she twists a thread back and forth
between her fingers. We wait
and my hedgehog heart curls up.

I want her to be happy I want her
to know me. This will not happen.
I watch the loose strand turn
in her hands. Minutes pass.

There's salt and a hint of rawness
in the wind. I begin to count
the paving stones between us.
They've always been there.

Now the bus comes slowly
rocking and rumbling up the street.
This is the last stop. The door opens.
We board and go home.

IV

It's teatime at the kitchen table,
part of our yearly visit.
We live on different continents.

The table is set. Everything is there
that should be there—familiar spoons,
cups and saucers. Mother's eyes

narrow. She looks up and says
I was not a good mother. Then she waits.
For confirmation? My disclaimer?

For the dusk to deepen? We know
what we know of each other—her squint
the thumb raised to frame, eliminate, or

propose changes, and so to see
the absent necessity that must be
brought to life or to the canvas

—ochre curve, red dab, blue daring dash.
Mother navigates her wheel of color
to find, by small signals of cell and eye,

what must be put there and what must not,
what, lost in her passion, she might find.
She hears and sees the red elegance,

the carnelian density. Deep ebony. Richness
she reaches as she steps back and forth—
the paintbrush hovers like a hummingbird's bill

as she feeds on color, drunk with it. I smell linseed.
My words find a way through the turpentine.
You taught me your love, I say. Mother nods.

It is that, though we mean it differently.
It's almost night. Blue cadmium light spans the table
between us and fills the white china cups.

V

I draw aside
the heavy curtain. Morning light
filters in from the veranda.
Glass doors stand open.

Below, vespas scream along the street.

In the next room
mother is dead
just a few hours. Sunlit
dust motes float in the air.

I must wait for a doctor, for standard procedures.

A cock screams in the distance.
Closer, keeping track of everything,
the minute hand of grandmother's blue clock
ticks and ticks.

VI

I buy tulips
to remember her,
swan flowers—
heads high,
arch gracefully in their vase.

As I watch
one red petal falls
heavily drifting.
But before that
drops have seeped down

on the table. Tears?
No, something more
visceral. Body fluid
pearling on the polished wood.
Corpses do it, too.

When they took mother
out of her bed
the pale stains were there
soaked into the hollow
of the white sheets.

So many hours later
was there still some heat?
They took her body away
but she had already left—
gliding out in her silver vase.

VII

A dark shadow skims toward me over gray water.
A bird touches the restless surface with each wing beat
and then settles as if weary. Only the neck and beak,
are visible and seem black like the handle to an iron pan.

Wave after wave my heart moves in grief.
I have lost an innocence I trusted
but somehow didn't even know I had, a faith
in loving. I believed my heart was fully given. Was it?

Now I see the bird sink out of sight
as if its body weighed too much.
Around the place it had been there is only lead-colored water.
I hear the foghorn again and again . . .
Will there be wings? Will there . . . . ?

VIII

The smell of vinegar, printers-ink and paper
hangs like a cloud around me. This cold spring afternoon
I am back home washing the windows—old news in my hands.

I am scrubbing the grief of many seasons away.
It's quiet in the neighborhood. The watchful dogs are asleep.
Little by little the glass turns transparent and luminous

as if it were not there at all. I want to grow old this way—
no illusions or self-accusations covering the view, no regrets
at last. Nothing to defend against, not even against

the light that has increased and pours down, becoming
almost painful. My shoulders ache as I scrub at my failures,
at longings that I never lived, at the love that I didn't give

or get when I could. Round and round my hands rub at the truth.
Full of grime the used newsprint shreds and drops from my hands.
Slowly a softening . . . the shimmer of blue evening light.

THEN, IS IT NOW?

The underbrush has been cleared.
The trees have grown taller.
Soon some will be marked and felled as
lumber. I have walked here for years
in their silence. They've stood their ground

and grown while I've wandered and
let the forest teach me what it can.
Meandering, the deer know the place well
and make their own paths to find water.
I follow them. Their white tails wave

like handkerchiefs in the dark or perhaps
like peace flags. I love these continual crossings
over old ground holding to the one task:
to stay awake until dawn. It's hard
to explain how this saves everything.

Reckoning

I take the white, sea-tumbled stone
from its shelf near the screen door.
It has always fit in the hollow of my hand

Near by is an earthenware bowl, full of peaches.

Red rocker by the window
and beside it, the hassock with black binoculars.
the latest precision in lenses.

There I am, in an old bedspread,

soft and yellow, cut and stitched by hand
into a loose gown I easily wear.
My hair is gray.

All my debts have been paid.

I take the binoculars from their case, focus.
As the tide comes in with its susurrus of memory
and water, I find myself again,

barelegged girl leaning down

as seawater slaps over our feet.
There is our stone—the one from the beginning.
Together we reach out and claim it.

Everything we ever needed is inside it.

ABOUT LOVE

SNAIL TIME

It's not too late.
Our bodies want to feel
the way the day dawns
in the skin slowly
with a blush.

Finding snail time
we glide over our lives,
a tender Braille
where joy is the thinnest layer
and asks everything.

DANCING

We are old now. The children's children
know it. Can't run. Can't skip rope.

Too much light hurts our eyes.

The waltz on the radio? Feet remember.
Rug rolls up on its own. Stumbling?

No matter. We both feel the sweep

and billow of the skirt, the taffeta rustle.
Our dance is banked like a fire.

Walls smoke. Paint curls on the ceiling.

This dance hall has no fire laws.
Let it burn.

THE BATH

Like old sea mammals, we slide
into the water, first one then the other.
Softly our fat folds around us
and we arrange ourselves to fit
under the surface as much as possible.

My breasts float loosely in the water and
your member is snuggled between my thighs.
We know how to be comfortable. No jets.
From time to time a drip from the faucet
is heard, and it is like our conversation.

Words rise out of a common silence
and emerge a drop at a time. This is
not idle. We are making something.
How long does it take for love to be
kind and slow? How long does it take

to not be afraid of nakedness,
of inner scars and imperfections,
allowing them to be visible places
where love wraps itself, the way
kelp wraps around rocks, softening

the edges and gaining a foothold?
We lie there long enough for
the water to cool before it gurgles
down and away. For a moment we wonder
how much longer we'll have to be together.

The thought is fleeting, but has come more
often of late. Now we towel each other
off. You pat my buttocks to get a move on,
affirming that sometimes small acts become
so tender they are too much to bear.

WORKING TOGETHER

I remember the gray treads that led from
the potting studio to the kitchen door—
aboriginal foot prints. They stop at the threshold.

Whatever was once wet and silent, tunneling
into clay to make space for emptiness
becomes domestic when my love enters the kitchen.

His blue, downtrodden work shoes
are left outside where they gape
side by side in rubbery surprise

at having been abandoned for this—
to be a husband chopping onions
and carrots in the kitchen with me.

Standing near him I smell the clay
and the liberty in him. Spotted with slip,
his shirt is an animal's skin.

I am outside of this. But I have seen
the perfectly round hole by the studio door
where a small creature has tunneled

into the moist earth to open
a still place under the foundation
below the potter's wheel as it spins.

I believe those two work together,
in a descending silence so deep
every thought sinks as a leaf does in a pond.

MAKEUP

We never thought this would happen.
Your pain is my Zen wall,
so huge it's turned into a billboard.
Your weathered face is plastered there.

Every morning I am harnessed and
climb into the bucket. The clips snap
and secure me. The winches squeal
and I am lifted up. By my feet

I have a can of blues, a quart of water
and some other colors. Now level
with your face, I am here to touch things up.
All day lowered and lifted to the pain.

I daub at the weathered cracks,
giving your teeth a flash of white,
your French beret another coat
of lasting black, your lips some gloss.

They are so dry I want to open them
and pour in water. There! I am sure
it will make things a little better and
make you smile. I want to imagine

your well being. We agree this is not
about endurance. Patience must become a light
that floods everything, and I am learning
there's no end to daubing. It is blood work.

Night comes around again. I am lowered to the ground,
step back needing distance to see you. Up there
you are gazing at the hopeless truth and I am falling
towards the bed, the unwashed brush still in my hand.

LOSING GROUND

In the dark you tell me
you are losing ground a little
every day. I nod. We are stumbling
along the narrow corridor
that leaves your skin cracked—
heels, thumbs and now an eyelid.
Your spine crumbles like bread,
but you are not leaving a trail,
and we are not yet lost in the woods.
Your pain shoots up to ten.
It takes a half an hour to pee.
But I see more that your eyes,
lighten when I come into the room,
and how a little smile plays across your face
before you say, Good Morning.
We are back again at the door
love means for us to open.

My Love in the Night

Legs wooden and heavy—so hard
to move from chair to chair.
Someone has to lift and guide.

The skin hangs in folds.
the way it does on an old elephant
in the zoo. Eyes black and deep,

that patience learned and relearned
at night when no one comes or remembers.
Yet, something inside is still moving

with a light silvery step it bounces
off this world, loves it—every dark corner
and moves without legs.

IN FEAR

I hold you. I hold you
for a moment. Let's dare
to feel how thick is the dark,
how covered with fur.

Could we lay our heads
here? Just for a moment
could we breathe?
Could we breathe the living beast?

CARE

I don't mean to be mean.
It just happens the way
a rubber band breaks
for being stretched beyond
its known self—a sudden snap,
a smarting release, and I have lost
myself as I know me. Branches break

in high winds not heeding how
they fall. Water surges over the banks
when the river cannot hold it.
This is not personal. Perhaps
this is the way we die
in little ways all the time until
our bodies will not contain us anymore.

Asked to be more than we can be
we snap, and are abducted
to some enormous distance, a vastness
without end. We zoom into the place
we have avoided where everything is
strange and severed. We try to live there
as if it were normal.

A Home Without a Basement

When I was small it was a passion, making rooms
and beds out of cardboard, hanging tiny pictures
of frogs on the walls, laying scraps of cloth
on floors and tables. The place thrummed.
I could always reach in and make things better
for the little plastic family I lived with.
We were safe in that home without basement.

Now I climb the spiral staircase in the whelk,
take naps in the nests left by finches, mud-daubed
and prickly. The mole hole is mine—a darkness
I don't clean. I've stopped making things better.
Instead I kiss the whiskered lips of my life's dear friend,
each time as if it were the last. The cardboard fell
down long ago. I am learning to tremble.

WHAT IF

What If we could trust
the basic love that each has
for themselves and only be concerned
when one of us stops that caring?

What if we let go of worry . . .
how we fit together or don't
as we age and lose, and what if
we ceased imagining dark futures?

We could be stars in a vastness
more intimate than breath. We'd be part of
one another the way color is part of
the spectrum. We would rest in light.

IF I COULD WRITE TO YOU

not a letter—I mean a slow tracing
the way a snail moves and leaves
evidence behind of having been there,
something visceral, I would write
with invisible ink on your body
that it is now unbearable not to love you,
and I wish sometimes there was a moment
of choice, but I am only able to see
the next little patch of skin breaking down
on your back and your bottom, and I can't help
beginning again without doubt to write
my body in yours.

NOONTIME

The sun streams across our luncheon table.
Soup and silence. My love sits close to me.
Clink of spoons against earthenware.

Peaceful and familiar these years of lunch.
Too simple the salty broth? The crumbs
scattered around the loaf we share? No.

You look up and I notice the blue rim
of the new cornea taken from the motorcycle boy
who landed in a ditch. It's stitched into the soft brown

of your eye. Here the visible truth—how
we need light from each other and yearn for
the gaze that doesn't shrivel, that regards what it sees.

Holding the Moment

I want to retrieve something transparent
—a smooth clear goblet.
Inside: red wine, dark like blood and fragrant.

I remember your hand holding the glass,

fingers careful, muscular and solid.
The room was amber, lit by the evening
light reflected from the garden wall,

golden and warm as apricots. It was August.
We were young and naked. My eyes darkened
with desire. We gazed at one another, holding the moment

as if we lived within a painting we could keep . . .

No one else was there. We could see
the soft blue folds of the open curtains.
For a long time we didn't move, knowing

that soon everything would be changed,
soon we would drink the cup, we would open.
We would die and open.

CLOSE

In the sofa again with our morning
tea, having been apart throughout
a long night. Where do we go
when we are not here?

Your hand wants to find me.
It seeks my heat under the nightgown,
under the heavy blanket of absence.
We lean into each other and dream

the dream of no body, the feel of
slipping out of our elderly skins,
out of the house and our history,
out of the night and the day

where we go when we are so near
one another that we are nowhere
and yet here—not even ourselves.
Yes, that close.

DURING A DARK TIME

I dreamt we were already dead
under a flowering tree. Spring leaves
were just beginning to open their sheer,
tender green. We were surprised
that our bodies were lighter than air.
We were free. Dying had been all anticipation,
a chill and terror to nurture. But
being dead turned out to be easy—

a kind solution. To seal it you gave me
almonds in oil. I think it was olive, sacred
to something human and very old that we'd
loved long ago. The taste filled me with tears.
It was soil I swallowed—the grit, the dense,
bitter taste of earth, the hurtful joy of it.
I woke in that bed, solid and sure again
we'd always somehow choose life.

NAKED

My arm flung over you
lifts and sinks
with each breath

Darkness presses in close.

The window is open
Flashes from thunderheads
light up our room

I see how small we are
side by side
in the marriage bed

So fragile

Against my arm your hair
feels soft   a slight dampness
where we touch   heat lingers

I know you are my brother at sea
my husband rising and falling
my friend without life-raft

We are always only here

About Love

Fog hugs the cedars, visible breath
as if some large beast were exhaling.
I stumble around,
hands in front of me. Fog,
I am soft in it—myopic
and suddenly slower. Could this be
the speed of kindness or
just simple courtesy? Am I able

to see you or is it rather that I feel
my way—finger tips resting on textures,
the physical letters of the world?
How do I know you?
White thickness hangs in the middle distance,
sweeps me around, brings me to your side,
one letter at a time. I touch so blindly
that I find you all over again.

ON THE ROOF

The glow of the city is light years
away. We're on night watch
with nothing much but dark
trusting dark, tender
in the kinship of being.

It's like listening to listening.

No stars. Quiet
unknowing keeps us together
in a gypsy music. One viola
and seven violins.
Infectious laughter. Ache.

All the while the doves on the roof's edge

invite us deeper into night—a flock
of white prayers cooing
and whispering, *Sursum
corda . . . Sursum corda,**
opening their wings.

**Lift up your heart.*

EVERY DAY

THE STOOP

I sit on the stoop,
the door closed behind me.

What do I wait for when
I have knocked for days without answer?

On the street children are playing.
Their high squeals rise like bubbles

in the morning air. Bursting.
These kids are not waiting.

I lean against the sunlit door.
Could it be that I am already inside

whatever matters, and that the stoop
is a place for the afternoon to settle,

languid and feline—
curling into my lap?

The Path Inside

How did this begin—a path
opening inside me from there to here?
It was in a thicket of trees, thorns,
and the soft footfalls of a deer picking her way
to berries and water. Both of us shy,
but not in a hurry. Mimicking the shadows
around us we melt, grazing in and out of light.

I think other deer follow, leisurely chewing
young leaves. Their munching is gentle and slow.
By coming here often our hoof prints deepen a path.
Above us breezes scuttle in the canopy of ash and alder.
How many times have I imagined walking here
to be made all over again, to see the moss grow
over boulders, steadily greening even on stone.

LIFTING INTO MORNING

It was a starling, I think
fallen out of its nest, stunned
but alive. It lay in my hands.
and didn't move. Wind came
to lift the belly feathers. Downy brown
and gray, there were layers of them
by the thin legs, curled now like commas.

One black eye looked at me—not in fear
nor resignation. I gazed back feeling
that warm, little life with its story inside—
the heart beating fast. I thought what courage
it takes to be with another—not wanting
or expecting anything—not afraid,
allowing what comes . . .

I watched as the fledgling stirred,
sat up on its tiny feet and shivered.
Done with its fall, sharp toes dug
into my hand and pushed off. Lifting,
lifting into morning, the bird hovered
and we flew.

AT WATER'S EDGE

Slap! Slap! The sea breaks against the boulders.
I'm here at water's edge drawn to the lapping,
to repetition—that moment when sameness opens
its wise doors, and I escape my own confinement.

How tenderly everything comes towards me then.
Water licks my hand, tastes me, loves me.
Beach plums turn on their orange lanterns.
Swallows pencil the sky with quick, silver poems—

wordless gestures of welcome. The grace-filled
phragmites bow their feathered heads patiently waiting
for the wind to give them a song. I root my body beside them.
We tremble with eagerness for something real to begin in us.

THE ROAD FLOWS OVER A HILL

The season's grief lies scattered on the shoulder of the road.
Each day we bring our sacks to pick up what debris we can.
The road flows over a hill we cannot see beyond.
Travelers whiz by in their speeding cars. They are faceless.

Sometimes they wave. Sometimes they slow a bit. And sometimes
there is too much left with a life of its own in the scrubby grass
between sumac and forgetting. We stop to mop our faces.

We are clearing more than what has been discarded.
Above us a falcon rises on a thermal and circles, weaving
another tale high in the treetops. The wings barely move
so full are they of silence and fierce benediction.

PASSION

Out in the fields the green wheat
reaches skyward, heavy with seed.
It has rained recently and the wet body
of the earth smells musty and metallic.

We are in line at the bakery. The fragrance
of fresh bread wraps around us.
We buy our baguettes. In each loaf
there is a kindness we want to live inside.

To have it, we tear things apart. I love you to pieces.
Rain, sun, sweat, the very ground—my knife spreads them
like butter on bread. I could eat you up. The world melts
on our tongues. Take. Eat. Do this. Remember.

SILENCE, THE RESCUE DOG

At night I hear scuffling. He comes to the bed,
jumps up on clean, newly washed sheets. I smell grass
rotting fruit, fur matted by rain. Slowly he licks my face.
In the moonlight the paw prints on my chest
attest to how much my heart has been touched.

The blinds are up and the window is open. We do not howl.
We do not sing. We forget everything we have ever said
and sit by the window seeing how the sill extends into darkness.
The mongrel shines in the silver light—a lord of life.
So quietly am I joined to all that is kind.

WINTER BREATH

A few leaves linger on the Japanese maple.
Doors are firmly shut and storms come
out of the cellar. We're in the box of winter.
Every year the cold brings it's questions,

questions I sense I must answer
and place my heart against the chill
to listen to my life blood pumping
with an ancient, human joy. It's high time

to be happy. Starlings puff out their feathers,
keeping warm. Huddled close they are alive
with little gray events and chatter from the railing
of the porch or scrabble for food beneath the tangled

branches of the leafless lilac. My winter breath
hangs in the air and disperses in the pale light.
Night creeps further into the day, comes up
the wooden stairs. I feel it licking my feet.

HIBERNATING

Like cloth the quiet falls
into place, falls white upon white,
covering my sleep. The silence

is dense—a brocade, rich cashmere
or fine merino, layering up and I begin
to feel the patterns of my breath

shuttling back and forth—constant
back and forth weaving up days
and hours, weaving a marriage gown

in which I wed myself to my life,
to have and to hold through all my winters
until love becomes lived.

WEDDING TWO PLACES

I think. No,
that's not entirely true.
I go off and find myself
in the back room at the top
of the stairs where the sun slants
in on the bed with the sunflower
in the middle of the coverlet.

There's a slight smell of mildew,
but when I open the window
the old lilac comes into the room
wearing her recent purple—
a scent sweet as blood. I love
the old wide boards, the hooked rug

and the flies stuck between the screen
and the window. No need for thinking here
because the room is complete down to the old
paperbacks, the used pencils, the uncompleted
puzzles and the Bible in its straw basket.
Maybe this is heaven, being overhead
in the attic, away but connected.

No one knows I am here so when
the door bell rings or the telephone jingles
I try to answer, to make conversation
as usual, maybe lunch and supper as well.
Meanwhile I am still upstairs somehow
sprawled on the bed with the sunflower
spreading its gold through my body.

I am growing old, unfolding petals.
Some have fallen away. But plenty of seeds remain
packed solidly together in honeycomb fashion.
In this abundance there is no end to sunflowers,
and no end to whatever I may think is an end.
So since unfolding is enough I've stopped thinking

about thinking because it's really just one
slightly dilapidated house. The doors stick
after weeks of rain. There is water in the well,
tested often. You can drink your fill
and are welcome to come and go as you please.
I do.

Rainy Invitation

Spring rain shrinks the house.
The walls turn inward
seeking warmth and light.
I silence the radio
not to crowd that dark corner

where vastness begins
and amplitude beckons
with a fat, curling finger.
Okay. The house lifts up
hovers over its founding stones,

rises past early leaves—
lime green on their slick, dark branches.
Rises far beyond the purple violets,
above the yard and the neighborhood
hiding in moss and shade.

Staked to the ground, dogs bark
and bellow, tugging on their chains.
But the house, heavy improbable bird,
is free in the wet and wild
amen.

SPRAY

Haze on the horizon. Far out
a fog horn bleats like a lost sheep.

A black butterfly hovers near my foot,
then weaves through the dune grass

as I walk. Sand trickles slowly down
to something wet and ancient. Nearby

in the water the ochre seaweed lifts and settles
as if someone were breathing from below.

The sun breaks through and I see that the stones
have moved further into the water. I've come

to be near these boulders, to be washed through.
Is there a better prayer than being soaked in beauty?

Now the black butterfly disappears in the blue shadows
of the beach roses. My eyes follow until its dark wings melt

into deeper darkness. It's noon. Church bells ring.
Wind throws a froth of spume into the air.

SNEAKERS

They hang on the electric wire above the road—a pair
of high-topped basketball sneakers dangling by their knotted laces.

How many tosses did some boy take in the dark with no one looking
to finally snag the wire? The sense of satisfaction must have been

wonderful, to have done something entirely useless with panache—
never mind propriety, the general good or warnings from authorities.

Each time he goes down the street now, there they are on high,
and he's pleased to know that he is responsible, and no one else knows.

No one looks up anyway. That is why having something
uplifting beyond what is determined by others is so delicious.

I love those sneakers, the way they swing lazily in the breeze
confirming that just being up there (or wherever) really matters.

LATE MORNING
AT THE RETREAT CENTER

Side by side two mallards sit on a stone,
iridescent jewels in a seaweed ring.
They are close to one another and so still
I want to be there tucked between their bodies.
Slowly the water rises and the ducks float off
their granite perch into the tide, pulling it
under them with their broad, orange feet.
I love this slow sculling and watch
how buoyed up they are having
what they need and possessing nothing.

Now the noon bell rings. Somewhere lunch
is being served on paper plates. There's small talk:
pass the salt, the ketchup and seconds please.
I am missing all that, recumbent on my rock
listening to the fog horn moan far away
though it is a halcyon day without a cloud
and so no need for navigation.
The sound fills me and I float,
drawn out of the shallows, out
of my body, out into everything.

IN THE BOSTON MUSEUM OF FINE ARTS

I saw a little cup, one I could hold in one hand
and the thumb would still meet the fingers, a cup
with ridges where I could feel how the potter shaped
the whirling clay. In a way I still hold his hand—
someone I have always known but lost
a hundred years ago. Haven't I always been
bound to the patient layers of earth, to silent deposits
where if I dig far enough I'm in common ground?
I love the light in the ancient glaze—celadon right to the rim
—asking, lip to lip. that I drink quietly and deep?

AT BOTTOM

Into the cove the river runs
to meet incoming water. Salt
and fresh mingle. It's low tide.
I can see bottom.

Slowly now, inching along the granite
ledge where the rock has turned pink
and white, marked by the tugging moon,
the tide pulses in—a rhythm

I can trust as blood flowing
to the heart. Here I feed
like an open mussel
hidden in river silt—

so simply then does
the iridescent light grow
silent and larger
from the inside out.

I Can't Tell You What Happened

Sometimes a dreadful happiness happens. Last night it came
because I left my mind's door unlatched, not on purpose, but
having been far too long in heartless routines I forgot the usual

shuttering. The latch didn't close, so later the wind opened a door
in my dream and let me out into night—a creature in heat
taking her chances with moonless possibilities. I can't tell you

what happened except that it was not yet morning when I woke
and smelled of grass and the deep stink of something wild. Disheveled
I was back, overcome, muddy and kinder. My pillow was wet.

I must have spilled tears when the four velvet chambers
of my heart took me into darkness where I was loved
more than I thought could be bearable.

IN SEASON

The poppy finally opens. Breath-
taking. Long days rooting down.
The ache grows and the furry pod
cracks bit by bit.

Glimpses of flaming taffeta.
Orange petals unfurl
and the purple-black center
covers me with fine dust.

This is not opium but
the pod's star-scattering beauty.
Soon tatters lie strewn on the ground.
I am ravished. So quietly silence creates me again.

LIKE A PEACE FLAG

Every day bursts open, shimmering
milkweed out of the casing.
I want to catch it. Without words

how do I say that my body is potent,
a pod full of joy, that while doing
simple things like cutting bread or

passing the butter, something breaks open
and I am suddenly lifted into air,
like a seed given over to weather and wind?

Carried, I float, dip, and twirling,
not caring if I'm snagged by gorse or
a wild rose and left all day fluttering . . .

...

MATURING ON THE SWING

To be as high as a kite or
a cloud is what I wanted as a kid
pumping the swing
with all my might,
toes seeming to touch tree tops
when the swing reached the height of its arc.

I never looked back
but used the inevitable
back swing to move forward
again, every muscle striving
to go beyond
the limitation of the heavy chains
and so to touch sky.

The longing was strong.
I wonder now if it was
God that I wanted,
a confirmation
of something bigger than
the tedium of being
too young to be considered.

I still crave that toe-touching feeling,
but now, my feet are planted
on the ground, I do not look up.
The sky has fallen
and I don't see very well.
Walking among these descended
clouds, I feel the soles of my feet
confirmed by everything that is earth.

RAIN

I feel the poem
of my life begin again
in the soft patter
of the rain at dawn
as it tip toes across the roof
and wants to be acknowledged
from outside
but not confined
by too much interiority
so that, the astonishing distance
between not this and not that
allows for a common air—
moist like slick birthing balm
coating everything
with reassurance—every blade of grass,
every shivering leaf, every
grey, abandoned stone and so
that no matter the circumstances
I am somehow lifted
above the ground and its gravity
over swamps and tundra,
over deserts and plains, over
icy roads, pain and the black numbing tarmac
of parking lots and grief,
and set adrift like a cloud,
out to sea, gathering
the experience of dissolution
where nothing can be done

but the pouring
of oneself back
down again
into everything,
into the density that is
not this, nor that
but a stumbling freedom
washed through
with rain-glazed immensities.

Thanks to the following journals
where some of these poems first appeared.

Lyric Recovery, "Gate Swiging"
Potomac Review, "Observation"
Pentimento, "Makeup"
The Wayfarer, "Noontime," "Rainy Invitation" and "Spray"
Snapdragon, "During A Hard Time"
Lalitumba, "On the Roof"
Sufi Journal, "The Road Flows Over A Hill"
The Contemplative Journal, "The Stoop," "At Water's Edge"
                                   and "Snail Time"
Common Ground, "Wedding Two Places"
Third Wednesday, "Sneakers"
Embracing the Seasons, "The Path Inside"
Earth's Daughters, "Stitching"

About the Author

Gunilla Norris' parents were world travelers in the Swedish diplomatic corps and so she grew up essentially in three places—Argentina, Sweden and the United States. As a child she was given a rich exposure to different languages and cultures.

She received her B.A. from Sarah Lawrence College and her M.S. from Bridgeport University in the field of human development. She is a mother and a grandmother. She has been a psychotherapist in private practice for more than thirty years and has felt privileged to accompany many people on their journeys to growth and healing. Her special love has been teaching meditation and leading contemplative workshops of many kinds.

As a writer Gunilla has published eleven children's books, one book of poetry and eight books on spirituality including: *Being Home, Becoming Bread, Inviting Silence, A Mystic Garden, Simple Ways, Sheltered in the Heart,* and *Match.*

Reflecting on her success thus far she comments, "When I published Being Home in 1991 I did not know that I had begun a series of books on what I now call household spirituality, or the practice of spiritual awareness in the most mundane and simple of circumstances. Together these books seem to me to be like a crystal with many facets. They are part of one thing and yet shed light from different perspectives on the humblest of our day-to-day tasks. It has always been my understanding that when we are really present in our daily activities, our lives become more luminous, filled with love and grace."

HOMEBOUND
PUBLICATIONS

Ensuring the mainstream isn't the only stream.

At Homebound Publications, we publish books written by independent voices for independent minds. Our titles focus on a return to simplicity and balance, connection to the earth and each other, and the search for meaning and authenticity. As an independent publisher we strive to ensure, "That the mainstream is not the only stream."

It is our intention at Homebound Publications to preserve contemplative storytelling. We publish full-length introspective works of creative non-fiction, essay collections, travel writing, and novels. In all our titles, our intention is to introduce new perspectives that will directly aid humankind in the trials we face at present as a global village.

So often in this age of commerce, entertainment supersedes growth; books of lesser integrity but higher marketability are chosen over those with much-needed truth but a smaller audience. Here at Homebound Publications, we focus on the quality of the truth and insight present within a project before any other considerations.

CPSIA information can be obtained
at www.ICGtesting.com
Printed in the USA
LVHW052246040523
746184LV00004B/197

9 781938 846656